105040 315

CARLOCK SCHOOL IMC

P9-CRK-934

THE CIVIL RIGHTS MOVEMENT
THE HISTORY OF BLACK PEOPLE IN AMERICA
1930-1980

Written by:
Stuart Kallen

McLean County Unit #5
Carlock IMC - 105

THE CIVIL RIGHTS MOVEMENT
A History of Black People in America 1930-1980

Published by Abdo & Daughters, 4940 Viking Dr., Suite 622, Edina, Minnesota
55435

Library bound edition distributed by Rockbottom Books, Pentagon Tower, P.O.
Box 36036, Minneapolis, Minnesota 55435

Copyright© 1990 by Abdo Consulting Group, Inc., Pentagon Tower, P.O. Box
36036, Minneapolis, Minnesota 55435. International copyrights reserved in all
countries. No part of this book may be reproduced in any form without written
permission from the publisher. Printed in the United States.

Library of Congress Number: 90-083619   ISBN: 1-56239-020-1

Cover Illustrations by: Marlene Kallen
Inside Photos by: Globe Photos
                  Bettmann Archive
                  AP/Wide World Photos

Reprinted 1993 by Abdo & Daughters.

Cover Illustrations by: Marlene Kallen

Edited by: Rosemary Wallner

TABLE OF CONTENTS

INTRODUCTION

This book explores the years when black people fought for the most basic rights guaranteed to white people in the Constitution of the United States. Some of the terms used can be confusing, so a glossary is presented here. (The definitions given are in relation to the black struggle and not necessarily the complete meaning of the word.)

CIVIL RIGHTS — The rights of black people to be treated equally with white people.

DISCRIMINATE — To deny someone equal rights because of their skin color (race).

INTEGRATE — To allow black people into the same areas used by white people. Example: Many people fought to integrate the schools in Arkansas.

PREJUDICE — Hatred or dislike of someone because of their race or beliefs. Judging someone because of their race.

RACISM — Same as prejudice.

SEGREGATE — To keep blacks separate from whites. Example: Many people wanted to segregate black people on buses. Black people fought segregation. They did not want to be segregated. Note: Desegregation is the same as integration.

Leaders of the civil rights movement both black and white, locked arms and led a march through Washington, D.C., on August 28, 1963, to fight racism and segregation.

CHAPTER 1
THE DEPRESSION YEARS

Last Hired — First Fired

Months before the stock market crashed in October 1929, many black people knew that something was wrong with the economy. Every day, newspapers in the black community, like the *Chicago Defender,* wrote about massive layoffs of black workers. Black workers summed up their situation with the statement, "I'm the last to be hired and the first to be fired." They did not need a newspaper to tell them something was wrong.

The booming economy of the twenties gave some black people the opportunity to advance themselves with decent jobs. When the stock market crashed, the country plunged into the most severe economic depression in United States history. By 1931, one out of every three blacks was unemployed. In cities like Atlanta, Georgia, and Norfolk, Virginia, 80 percent of the black people there were in need of public relief, or welfare. But relief was nowhere in sight. With 14 million white people out of work, the hardships of black people went unnoticed. Agencies that helped the poor had their resources stretched to the breaking point. For black people, the fight against discrimination had to be put on hold. Suddenly, there was a new enemy to fight —starvation.

It's hard to imagine discrimination in relief programs, but in the early 1930's, soup kitchens and shelters for homeless refused admission to blacks. When help was available in government programs, starving white people were given much larger relief checks than starving blacks. The gains that black people made during the twenties were swept aside as depression, disease, and discrimination took their toll on the black community.

The New Deal
Herbert Hoover, a Republican, was president during the first years of the Depression. Until that time, the Republican Party was the party that most black people voted for. It was started before the Civil War. Abraham Lincoln, the first Republican president, was considered by many blacks to be a hero for ending slavery.

The Democratic Party in the South had used the terror of the Ku Klux Klan to prevent blacks from voting.

In 1932, Hoover ran against Franklin Delano Roosevelt, a Democrat. Hoover had completely ignored the plight of blacks. Roosevelt made a special effort to reach black voters and help them. Most blacks decided to vote for "bread and butter instead of the memory of Abraham Lincoln." Roosevelt was elected and the New Deal began.

Roosevelt immediately set up agencies to relieve the effects of the Depression. He made sure that black people were included. The Works Progress Administration (WPA), the Civilian Conservation Corps (CCC), and other agencies gave hundreds of thousands of black people industrial training and opportunities to work. Roosevelt even set up agencies to employ writers, actors, musicians, and photographers. These organizations were also open to blacks. Many well-known black writers were employed by the Federal Writers Project. The Federal Theater sponsored many interracial and all-blak plays in cities all over the country. Black playwrights were asked to write for the Federal Theater.

The National Youth Administration (NYA) enrolled over 600,000 black children in its classes. Black adults also received educational help under other programs. By 1939, over 1 million black people had work skills learned from federal programs. Black schools, hospitals, community centers, and playgrounds were built by newly trained black workers in the Public Works Administration. Roosevelt was so popular that many black people called him the "Great White Father." In 1936 and in 1940, blacks voted overwhelmingly for Roosevelt.

Besides helping working-class blacks, Roosevelt welcomed college educated people into the highest reaches of government. In 1938, Roosevelt's "Black Cabinet" had over twenty specialists in almost every department of government, from the Department of Interior to the Department of Justice and the Department of Commerce. Roosevelt depended on these people to tell him what black people expected and wanted from the government. The cabinet members demanded equal opportunities for blacks. They helped black people feel that they were an important segment of American society.

Unfortunately, Roosevelt's acceptance of blacks could not change generations of discrimination throughout the huge federal government. Discrimination continued in many federal programs designed to help the poor. Racial violence against black people continued throughout the thirties. For the people who were the poorest segment of American society, the Depression made life even harder.

President Franklin D. Roosevelt worked hard to stop racism.

CHAPTER 2

THE BLACK STRUGGLE DURING WORLD WAR II

Demands for Equal Opportunity

In 1939, World War II started in Europe. Before the United States joined the fight in 1941, American industries worked overtime to supply the Allies with the materials for war. But defense plants with government contracts refused to employ black workers. The National Association for the Advancement of Colored People (NAACP) organized a march on Washington, D.C., to demand equal rights for black workers. The NAACP expected over 100,000 black people from across the country to protest in Washington, D.C., on June 1, 1941. President Roosevelt did not want the march to take place. Roosevelt promised action if the march was canceled. Black leaders called off the march. On June 25, Roosevelt signed Executive Order 8802. The order banned discrimination in industries holding government contracts. He also set up a Committee on Fair Employment Practices to make sure the order was obeyed.

Patriotism and Prejudice

In December 1941, the United States became involved in World War II in Europe and the Pacific. President Roosevelt said that the war was being fought for the Four Freedoms: freedom of speech, freedom of religion, freedom from want, and freedom from fear. Many black Americans rushed to join the fight for freedom. Often they had to fight bias at home before they could fight the enemy across the ocean.

There was strict segregation in the armed forces. Blacks were only allowed to work in the food services in the Navy. In the Army, blacks were kept in all-black units, many times with prejudiced white officers. They were denied admission into the Air Force and Marines. The American Red Cross even segregated the blood in its blood banks. When draft laws were passed requiring Americans to serve in the armed forces, many black leaders urged Roosevelt to stop discrimination. They wanted black recruits to be given the same training as whites. They also wanted blacks to be allowed to be officers. Black leaders also demanded that black doctors and nurses be integrated into the services.

The government took action. In 1941 the Army accepted blacks for unsegregated training. The Navy and Marines allowed blacks to join as equals. The Air Force opened a special post for the training of black pilots. Black women were also accepted. More than one million blacks served in World War II.

"Jim Crow" at Home

Over one hundred years before World War II, in 1831, a white singer painted his face black and sang a song called "Jump, Jim Crow." Black actors were not allowed to perform for whites, so many white actors painted their faces to look like black people. As a result of the song, "Jim Crow" became associated with segregation. Laws that made it illegal for black people to use white people's street cars, rest rooms, schools, parks, restaurants, water fountains, and other facilities were called Jim Crow laws.

During World War II, Jim Crow laws were still used widely in America. Black author Langston Hughes wrote, "Blacks who wanted to serve their country did so at the risk of their dignity and sometimes at the risk of their lives, long before they met the official enemy. The enemy that hurt them the worst was Jim Crow. Jim Crow ignored their citizenship and scorned them as human beings."

In most public places before the 1960's, segregation signs separated blacks and whites.

Thousands of black people moved to Northern cities to work in defense plants. More than 50,000 moved to Detroit in two years. Everywhere, housing became a problem for blacks. White people often opposed black people moving to their neighborhoods. Bombings, fires, violence, and forced evictions awaited many black families moving into white communities. Race riots broke out in Detroit, New York, Mobile, Alabama, Beaumont, Texas, and other cities.

Military centers were also the sights of riots. The military's efforts to end segregation were often met with resistance in towns where segregation had been the rule for decades. Many German prisoners of war were brought to American to be kept in Army prisons until the end of the war. The German prisoners in transit were allowed to eat at railway station restaurants while their black American guards could not. Blacks were also kept out of military recreational facilities.

Black people trying to get to work had other problems. Sometimes half-empty railway trains would not admit blacks if the all-black, Jim Crow car was full. Some buses would not even stop for blacks. Sometimes, black soldiers on leave could not even get home, or if they did, could not get back to camp on time.

CHAPTER 3

GIFTED BLACKS FROM THE THIRTIES AND FORTIES

In spite of the Depression, in spite of discrimination, in spite of poverty, many black people became well known for their distinguished achievements. In sports, literature, theater, science, the armed forces, and politics, thousands of black people overcame the odds and became tops in their field. Here are the stories of some black people who fought prejudice and won.

Joe Louis — 1914-1981 — Boxer

Joe Louis represented the hopes and dreams of black people during the Depression. He rose out of poverty to become the Heavyweight Boxing Champion of the world. When Joe Louis won again and again, millions of black people felt the victory.

Joe Louis Barrow was born in a one-room shack in Chamber County, Alabama. By the age of four, Louis was already working in the cotton fields beside his mother and father. Louis did not learn to read or write until he was nine years old.

During his childhood, Louis's father died and his mother remarried Pat Brooks, who had five children. Pat went to Detroit to find work and eventually sent for his family. Louis was still poor, but in Detroit, he had indoor plumbing and electric lights.

When Louis was a teenager, he began to box. Although he was knocked down seven times during his first match, within two years he won forty-eight out of fifty-four fights. As an amateur heavyweight, he dropped the Barrow from his name and began to use the name Joe Louis.

In 1934, Louis decided to fight professionally. But he would have to fight discrimination outside the boxing ring first. Most white fighters would not fight a black man. Many times during interracial fights, riots broke out if the black man won.

By 1935, Louis was beating the odds. That year, he went into the ring with Primo Carnera, the "Man Mountain." At six feet six inches, Carnera provided quite a challenge to Louis. The fight was held at Yankee Stadium in New York. Over 1,500 policemen surrounded the stadium to prevent riots. When Louis knocked out Carnera in the eighth round, thousands of black people jammed the streets of Harlem, New York, to celebrate.

Joe Louis was the Heavyweight Boxing Champion of the world for eleven years.

The next year, Louis was scheduled to fight a German boxer, Max Schmeling. More than just an opponent, Schmeling represented Adolf Hitler's Germany. Hitler believed that German's were better than blacks and Schmeling would help prove it. Joe Louis represented black hope under American democracy. When Schmeling knocked out Louis in the twelfth round, hundreds of black pepole were seen openly weeping in the streets.

In 1937, Louis gained the heavyweight title when he beat James Braddock. In 1938, Louis fought Schmeling again and beat him in the first two minutes of the fight. Once again, millions of people celebrated the victory with Louis.

After four years in the army and a few more fights, Louis retired from boxing in 1949. In seventy-one fights, Louis had only been defeated three times. He was the heavyweight champion for eleven years, longer than any other fighter. Joe Louis was an inspiration to black people all over the country. His fame gave people a shining light in the darkness of the Depression.

Richard Wright — 1908-1960 — Author

Richard Wright is one of the most famous black novelists that the United States has ever produced. Born into a life of poverty and despair, Wright wrote about the suffering of black people. He shocked some Americans into changing their ways.

Richard Wright was born into desperate poverty in Tennessee. When he was four years old, he accidently started his house on fire and was beaten so badly that he almost died. Hunger and poverty were all that Wright knew as a boy. His father abandoned his family, and his mother put him and his brothers in an orphanage. Wright ran away but was returned to the orphanage. Soon he was sent to Arkansas to live with relatives.

Wright's uncle was murdered and his mother suffered a stroke, so he went to live with his grandmother in Jackson, Mississippi. In Jackson, Wright was allowed to attend school where he learned to read. His love of reading inspired him to be an author, but his grandparents discouraged him. They said that a black man could never make a living as an author.

Wright spent his years in Jackson working at menial jobs. In desperation, he stole a gun and some food. He sold the gun and bought a train ticket to Memphis. In Memphis, Wright worked in an optical shop. He borrowed a library card from a friendly white man and began reading whenever he could.

In 1927, Wright moved to Chicago. He worked at several jobs. When the Depression started, however, he found himself unemployed. In 1937, Wright moved to New York City, where his book of short stories was published. In 1940, Wright published *Native Son.* Within three weeks, the book sold over 250,000 copies and made Wright a famous author. *Native Son* told the harsh realities of prejudice in the North and how they affected a young black man. Wright soon published *Twelve Million Black Voices* and *Black Boy,* a book about his terrible chidhood.

Wright moved to Paris and continued to write novels. He was considered one of the finest authors in the United States. His novels showed the world the real lives of poor black people in America. Millions of people benefited from the education that Richard Wright gave them in his books.

World famous author, Richard Wright.

Paul Robeson — 1898-1976 — Actor

Robeson was the first black awarded all-American status in football. He received a law degree at Columbia University in 1923, after only two years study. After graduation, Robeson was asked to star in several plays written by Eugene O'Neill. He soon became famous in the United States and Europe for his acting and singing abilities. Robeson starred in many Broadway plays including *Showboat* and Shakespeare's *Othello*. In the 1940's, Robeson was involved in civil rights protests, which led the U.S. Government to "blacklist" him. Theater owners and movie producers refused to hire him. The State Department revoked his passport, and he was unable to leave the country. Robeson's income went from 104,000 dollars a year in 1947 to 2,000 dollars a year after the blacklisting. The State Department returned his passport in 1958, but by then, illness had forced Robeson to quit singing and acting. He lived quietly in Harlem until his death in 1976.

American singer and actor, Paul Robeson.

Richard Drew — 1904-1950
Doctor, Scientist

Richard Drew was a surgeon and scientist who
first separated whole blood from blood plasma
during World War II. Drew knew that whole blood
spoils rapidly but plasma can be stored much
longer. Dr. Drew's process saved thousands of
lives because blood was available for people

wounded during the Nazi bombing of England in 1940. Drew was appointed director of the Red Cross program to collect blood for the U.S. Armed Forces. The military, however, would not accept black people's blood. When Drew protested, the military agreed to accept black people's blood but insisted that it be kept separate from white people's blood. This racist policy caused Drew to resign from the program. Drew was killed in a car accident in 1950.

Jackie Robinson — 1919-1972
Baseball Player

Jackie Robinson was the first student to win letters at four different sports (basketball, baseball, football, and track). He won them at the University of California in Los Angeles in 1940. Robinson was drafted in 1941 but was denied admission to officer's school because he was black. His protests caused the military to start training black officers. After the war, in 1945, Robinson was asked to join the Brooklyn Dodgers baseball team. After playing in the Minor League for a year, Robinson became the first black Major League baseball player in 1947. Many of his teammates signed a petition to have him removed from the team. The Philadelphia Phillies and the St. Louis Cardinals threatened a strike and refused to play against Robinson and his team. The National League President, Ford Frick, supported Robinson. In 1947, with Robinson's help, the Dodgers won the National League pennant. Robinson was the first black man to play in a World Series that year. He was named Rookie of the Year in 1949 and admitted to the Baseball Hall of Fame in 1962, the first year that he was eligible.

Baseball Hall of Famer, Jackie Robinson.

CHAPTER 4
OPEN UP THE SCHOOLHOUSE

Many thousands of black people gave their lives to fight Hitler's racism in Europe during World War II. When the fight was over, blacks in the United States still faced the same Jim Crow laws, the same poor quality schools, the same discrimination in housing, and the same racial prejudice as before. In Alabama, Texas, Georgia, Mississippi, South Carolina, and other southern states, most black people were still denied the right to vote. In 1948, blacks were allowed to vote in the South Carolina primaries for the first time since 1877! Murder and terror still kept blacks away from the polls. Black taxpayers were not allowed to attend state supported universities in the early 1950's.

Black people found a friend in President Harry S. Truman. When Truman ran for vice-president in 1944, he supported a federal antilynching bill, fair employment practices, and equal voting rights for blacks. When Truman became president in 1945, he established a committee on civil rights to study the problems black people faced in the United States. The committee found many serious problems and explained them in detail. In his 1948 State of the Union address, Truman became the first president ever to set a national goal for securing "full human rights" for black people. Truman also became the first president to ask for legislation ending discrimination in employment and transportation facilities.

United States President Harry S. Truman (1945-1953).

Unfortunately, Congress refused to enact a federal antilynching bill or any other of Truman's requests. Some states, however, enacted bills of their own. By 1948, some northern states officially outlawed discrimination in housing, schools, public transportation, restaurants, and theaters. These laws were not faithfully enforced in many cases. In the 1940's, black people began turning to the United States Supreme Court to give them the rights guaranteed to them in the Constitution.

"Separate But Equal"

Since 1896, black people lived under the "separate but equal" laws enacted in many states. In that year, the Supreme Court said black people could be kept separated from whites in schools, train cars, and other places, as long as equal facilities were provided for blacks. Jim Crow laws were enacted that kept black people separated from whites, but their facilities were never equal. In the South, most state governments spent ten times more money educating white students. Black schools were usually run-down shacks with few books and supplies. Black facilities, whether schools, train cars, or public rest rooms, were almost always inferior to white facilities. Until 1954, black people were kept separate, but their accommodations were not equal.

The Battle Over Schools

On May 17, 1954, the Supreme Court ruled that the "separate but equal" doctrine was illegal in education. It said that black children were allowed to go to the same schools as white children. Two weeks later, the Court ordered seventeen states with separate but equal schools to integrate them immediately. One year later, the Court said the ruling also applied to tax supported colleges and universities.

The Supreme Court decisions started a battle unlike any other since the Civil War. The governors of South Carolina, Georgia, and Mississippi threatened to abolish public schools before they would let blacks and whites attend the same classes. One hundred senators and congressmen from the South signed a petition against the ruling. In Virginia, white politicians, ministers, and others threatened "massive resistance" to school integration. Racist hate groups formed to protest the decision. In many states, politicians made laws with loopholes designed to defeat the court-ordered integrations. Some of these laws kept black students out of white schools for ten years. Many black people realized that noble words on paper could not change the reality of discrimination they faced daily.

The Fight in Arkansas

In September 1957, nine black students went to their first day of school at Central High in Little Rock, Arkansas. It took a Supreme Court decision, a presidential proclamation, the 101st Airborne Division of the U.S. Army, and the Arkansas State Militia to allow them to attend. After two years of long and complicated battles those students were permitted entrance to the school.

The battle to let the students enter Central High had begun two years earlier. In 1955, Daisy Bates, a black newspaper publisher from Little Rock, organized a campaign to let nine students attend the all-white Central High. The windows of her home were broken by rock-throwing mobs. Her house was sprayed by bullets and crosses were burned on her lawn. The school board offices were bombed. Forty-four teachers who favored integration were fired. Mrs. Bates's newspaper was forced to close. For two years, racists used violence to make their point.

On September 5, 1957, National Guardsmen enforce segregation against the "Little Rock Nine" by not letting the black students enter school.

33

The Governor Blocks the Doors

On September 5, 1957, the governor of Arkansas, Orval Faubus, posted the Arkansas National Guard in front of Central High to keep the black students out. White mobs outside the school threatened the lives of the blacks while police ignored the violence. As the National Guard blocked the school's entrance with their rifles, racists in the crowd yelled obscenites and called for lynchings. Several of the black teenage students barely escaped with their lives. No black students went to Central High School that day.

For many weeks, a battle was waged in several courtrooms. Faubus was ordered to remove the National Guard from the school. President Dwight Eisenhower met with the governor and asked him to allow the black students admission. The Justice Department ordered Faubus to desegregate, but Faubus stood firm.

On September 23, the Little Rock Nine, as the students are called, tried to go to school again. Four black reporters went with them. Police cars carrying the students and reporter arrived at the school seconds before the 8:45 bell rang. The crowd thought the black reporters were the student's parents, and immediately attacked them. Three of the reporters ran away, but Alex Wilson of the *Chicago Defender* was hit in the head with a brick. The six-foot tall ex-Marine went down hard as the police watched, refusing to help him. Meanwhile, the nine students sneaked in the side door of the school. When the mob realized what had happened, they turned their anger on the white reporters who were there. Journalists and photographers from *Life* magazine were beaten and their cameras destroyed. People in the mob screamed, cursed, and wept as the black students looked out the school windows.

Calling Out the Army

That evening, Eisenhower ordered the 101st Airborne Division to Little Rock. He went on national television to explain his decision to use federal troops. On September 24, 350 paratroopers stood in front of Central High. A convoy of jeeps with machine guns transported the children to school. Helicopters circled overhead as the students climbed the steps into the school. Once inside, each student was given a bodyguard. At the end of the day, each student was escorted home.

White students shouted insults as a fifteen-year-old black student calmly walked toward the entrance of an all-white school.

Once in the school, some of the white students became friends with the black students. Blacks were invited to eat lunch with a group of whites. Several white students defended the blacks's rights to an equal education. Unfortunately, most of the black students spent the school year enduring name-calling, shoving, and tripping. Racist students even threw objects at the black students.

For the next several years, Orval Faubus tried to thwart the Supreme Court order by shutting the schools completely. Most white students attended private schools. Blacks had no schools to attend. But by 1962, Arkansas had integrated its schools.

In states like Mississippi, segregation was still enforced in 1962. When James Meredith, a twenty-nine-year-old Army veteran tried to attend the University of Mississippi, the governor of that state, Ross Barnett, personally blocked his way. Barnett said he would "die before he'd let any black students attend 'Ole Miss." It took 15,000 federal troops to permit Meredith to register for college. Riots on the campus injured hundreds and killed two men.

CHAPTER 5
MOVING TO THE FRONT

If black people did not like the separate seating arrangements at a movie theater or restaurant, they could choose not to spend their money at such places. But many black people had to use city buses to ride to and from work. And the discrimination practiced by southern bus companies was a daily fact of life for most black people until 1955.

In the South, if black people wanted to use city buses, they paid their fares at the front of the bus. Then they were forced to sit in a separate section at the back of the bus. When they exited the bus, they had to leave through the back doors. If the black section was full, black people had to stand even if there were empty seats in the white section. If the white section was full, black people had to give up their seats to white people. Many black people suffered the cruelties of prejudice in private. But thousands of blacks rode buses with whites everyday. Day after day, black people stood crowded together at the backs of buses, while the people that forced them to do that rode comfortably, right in front of them. Many people believe that this is why public buses were the first battleground in the fight for desegregation.

Rosa Parks Keeps Her Seat

Montgomery, Alabama, was a city where 40,000 black bus riders had to give up their seats to only 12,000 white riders. On December 1, 1955, Rosa Parks, a forty-three-year-old black woman, boarded a bus in Montgomery. Parks sat in the middle section of the bus where blacks were allowed to sit unless the white seats filled up. When several white men got on the bus, Parks was told by the bus driver to move so that the white men could have her seat. Parks refused and was arrested for violating the Jim Crow laws. In the jail cell, she desperately wanted water. But the police would not let her relieve her thirst because the drinking fountain was for "whites only."

News of Parks's arrest soon reached Edgar Daniel Nixon, a former head of the local NAACP. Nixon had been trying to stop Montgomery's bus discrimination for years. He wanted to organize black people to stop using the city bus system until the bus company treated blacks equally. If the bus company stopped receiving black rider's money, they would have to stop the discrimination. When a group of people refuse to use a certain product because they disagree with the company's policies, it is called a *boycott*.

When Parks was arrested, Nixon saw his chance. He called nineteen black ministers in Montgomery and organized a bus boycott. Over 35,000 flyers were printed and distributed by black college students. The flyers explained why Rosa Parks had been arrested. The flyers also asked every black person to stay off city buses for one day, Monday, December 5, the day Parks was to go to trial. The flyers circulated secretly through Montgomery's schools, bars, churches, and stores. Secrecy was important because people were afraid of losing their jobs or being lynched.

Rosa Parks is finger printed after her arrest for refusing to give up her seat to a white bus passenger.

Dr. King Steps In

On Monday, the buses were empty. Montgomery's eighteen black-owned taxi companies agreed to transport blacks for the same fare as the bus, ten cents. That night, in the churches, thousands of people gathered to rally against segregation. A new reverend in town, twenty-six-year-old Dr. Martin Luther King, Jr., gave a fiery speech to the boycotters. With thousands packed in churches and thousands more listening through loudspeakers in the streets, it was decided that the boycott would last until segregation ended. For the next thirteen months, empty buses drove through the streets of Montgomery.

Four days into the boycott, city officials declared that they would not give in to black demands. They threatened to fine black taxi drivers if they did not charge a minimum fare of forty-five cents. King went to work and organzied a car pool network where blacks with cars would take blacks without them to work. Many white employers offered their cars for support. King set up the Montgomery Improvement Association (MIA) to organize the boycott and collect funds. Before long, the MIA had forty-two pick-up points for the car pools.

Dr. Martin Luther King, Jr., explains to a group that the Alabama bus boycott will continue "no matter how many times they convict me."

On Janaury 30, King's house was firebombed. His wife, Coretta, hid in a back room with their seven-month-old baby. On February 1, Nixon's house was firebombed. He too escaped injuries. On February 12, King and twenty-four other ministers were arrested under a little-used Alabama law prohibiting boycotting. King was convicted and fined five hundred dollars. When he was released to appeal the case, King started touring the country to raise money for the boycott. Everywhere he went, people marveled at his beautiful and thoughtful speeches.

Victory!

The case against Rosa Parks finally went to the United States Supreme Court. The Court struck down the Jim Crow laws. On December 20, 1956, thirteen months after the boycott began, blacks once again started using the Montgomery bus system. This time they sat wherever they wanted. Soon blacks were also hired to be bus drivers.

Now a different kind of battle was being waged in Montgomery. White terrorists were shooting at buses and firebombing churches and homes of black people. But King continued to preach the message of nonviolence. Soon, he was organizing boycotts in cities all over the South.

CHAPTER 6
RIDING TO FREEDOM

"I sat-in at a restaurant for six months, and when they finally agreed to serve me, they didn't have what I wanted." — overheard at a sit-in demonstration, 1962.

By 1960, there was a new generation of black college students. These students had been brought up during the Little Rock school protests and the Montgomery bus boycott. While their parents may have settled for the Jim Crow way of life, these young people would not. In the wake of the bus boycott, new organizations were formed by Dr. King and others. The Southern Christian Leadership Conference (SCLC) and the Congress for Racial Equality (CORE) were two of the main groups teaching nonviolent protest to black students and others. Across the South, these organizations held sit-ins, boycotts, pickets, and protests.

When a restaurant refused to serve black students, they simply filled up the tables and sat there for hours until no white customers had room to sit down. When police arrested every protester at the counter, another group of protesters sat down. Wave after wave of protesters blocked the lunch counter until the jails were full. Before long, blacks were being served at restaurants.

After the sit-ins desegregated hundreds of restaurants in the South, black students started having read-ins at white libraries, wade-ins at white beaches, kneel-ins at white churches, and even sleep-ins at white hotels. The police responded by arresting hundreds of blacks. Police dogs bit protesters. Judges fined protesters huge amounts of money and gave them heavy prison sentences. White mobs with baseball bats and axe handles attacked youths. The black protesters were punched, pushed, and spit on by mobs in every city.

The sit-ins and boycotts worked. By the end of 1960, restaurants, theaters, hotels, department stores, and public facilities all over the South started dropping the "color barrier." Protesters that were arrested and imprisoned had their convictions thrown out by higher courts.

Freedom Riders   — Freedom Riders' song.
"I'm taking a ride on the Greyhound bus line.
I'm riding the front seat to Jackson this time.
Hallelujah, I'm traveling;
Hallelujah, ain't it fine?
Hallelujah I'm travling
Down Freedom's main line."

Four Jackson, Mississippi, blacks "sit-in" at a white drug store lunch counter as part of a move to crack the city's segregation barriers.

46

Public buses were the main form of transportation for blacks traveling from state to state in 1961. Unlike city buses that had been desegregated, interstate buses still discriminated against blacks. Bus stations had two waiting rooms, one for blacks and one for whites. Blacks also had separate ticket windows, bathrooms (if any), and lunch counters. When black students in the South got tired of this system, they decided to go on "freedom rides" to test bus, air, and rail lines. All were pledged to nonviolence.

Everywhere the freedom riders went in the deep South, they were met with violence. Racist mobs beat people, burned buses, and terrorized the black and white freedom riders. The police and National Guard units looked the other way. Many times, ambulance drivers and hospitals would not treat bleeding, wounded protesters. Many protesters were permanently disabled or killed during the freedom rides.

The problem got so bad that President John F. Kennedy and his brother Robert Kennedy (the Attorney General) had to step in. The President ordered official cooperation with the Freedom Riders. But that did not stop the governors of Alabama and Mississippi from having their police beat and arrest the riders. Many Freedom Riders were sent to maximum security prisons by prejudiced judges. Kennedy urged black voter registration. After awhile, blacks started voting in greater numbers, and a few prejudiced sheriffs and judges were voted out of office. When the buses were desegregated, the Freedom Riders went on to other projects.

The Birmingham Protests

The year 1963 was a hard one for Martin Luther King, Jr., and the SCLC. George Wallace, a strict segregationist had been elected governor of Alabama. Wallace stood in front of the doors to the University of Alabama and swore to keep blacks out of the college forever. The Federal Bureau of Investigation (FBI) under the leadership of J. Edgar Hoover tapped King's phone and opened his mail. King suffered some setbacks. His popularity was on the wane.

The year before, the city of Birmingham, Alabama, had closed sixty-eight parks, thirty-eight playgrounds, six swimming pools, and four golf courses to avoid integrating the facilities. Stores in Birmingham that had desegregated were hassled by building inspectors and other city officials. The officials wanted to bring back segregation.

Dr. King decided to make Birmingham, Alabama, the next target of SCLC's protests. Before the protests, King toured the country making speeches and raising money for bail and defense. King also organized children to protest, thinking the police would treat them with less hostility.

Children of Freedom

On May 2, 1963, about 1,000 black children ages six through eighteen marched in Birmingham. All of them were arrested and taken to Birmingham's jail. The next day 1,000 more children marched. The city's police chief, Bill Connor, brought out police dogs and firemen. Connor ordered the firemen to turn their firehoses on the children. With 100 pounds of pressure per square inch, the hoses hit the children with enough force to rip bark off of trees. Children were knocked down, thrown over cars and slammed against curbs. Several other children were attacked by dogs. That night, Americans all over the country saw Connor's brutality on the evening news. Soon the whole world saw the images.

Blacks in Birmingham were outraged. What had started as a nonviolent protest soon erupted into riots. The Ku Klux Klan bombed King's hotel. The Alabama State Police and the Birmingham city police attacked blacks with clubs, gas, and guns.

During the 1960's, policemen used dogs to attack civil rights demonstrators.

50

Stores were burned. The number of casualties mounted. Fearing that the rioting would spread across the entire country, President Kennedy had to take personal charge of the situation. Kennedy promised an end to segregation, and the rioting came to an end.

On June 19, 1963, Kennedy sent to Congress the strongest civil rights bill in history. The bill empowered the attorney general to end segregation in schools and cut off funds to schools that would not allow blacks. It also outlawed Southern laws that prohibited blacks from voting. Martin Luther King, Jr., wanted to make sure the bill passed. He wanted to demonstrate the power of black people. King decided to organize the biggest demonstration ever. King would take the cause to Washington, D.C.

CHAPTER 7

THE MARCH ON WASHINGTON

About 15,000 people had been arrested during the various fights for freedom nationwide. By the summer of 1963, blacks everywhere were ready to take to the streets to demand full equality.

Black organizations such as CORE, the SCLC, and others chose August 28 for a march on Washington. Many leaders expected a few thousand people. President Kennedy tried to get leaders to call off the march saying that the civil rights bill had a better chance of passage if blacks did not cause any trouble. Once Kennedy saw that the blacks would not call off the march, he gave his support. Many politicians in the Senate and Congress were opposed to the march and the black demands.

Two thousand freedom buses and thirty freedom trains brought blacks to Washington from all over the country. Hour after hour, people gathered at the Lincoln Memorial. The entire area between the Washington Monument and the Lincoln Memorial became a sea of people. The pond on the Mall had thousands of people wading in it to cool off from the summer's heat. By the end of the day, 250,000 black people and 60,000 white people had arrived to demand freedom and equal rights for black people. At the time, it was the largest demonstration in the history of the United States.

Dr. Martin Luther King, Jr., addressed thousands of blacks and whites who gathered in front of the Lincoln Memorial in a demonstration for civil rights.

Musical entertainers Bob Dylan, Joan Baez, Josh White, Odetta, Mahalia Jackson, and Peter, Paul and Mary sang to the crowd. Church leaders, labor representatives, and black activists made speeches. John Lewis, one of the leading speakers, electrified the crowd saying, "We shall splinter the segregated South into a thousand pieces, and put them back together in the image of God and democracy." Martin Luther King, Jr., gave his "I Have a Dream" speech. It was a speech of hope and determination. King called for love, racial harmony, and black and white living together in peace.

The March on Washington was a great success. There was no violence. Many Americans witnessed for the first time black and white people arm in arm, united, marching side by side. The eyes of the world, through television and newspapers, focused on black people and black problems. The march was the high point for millions of black people and helped push the "freedom train" a little further down the track.

CHAPTER 8
AFTER THE MARCH

Just eighteen days after the march, a bomb was thrown through a church window in Birmingham where black children were attending Bible class. Four children were killed. Once again, black people were reminded of the hard truth. The March on Washington was only one day in a long and continuing fight against racism. Hopes were further diminished when John F. Kennedy was assassinated in Dallas, Texas, on November 22, 1963. Kennedy had been a good friend to black people and his death slowed the civil rights legislation in Congress.

By 1965, President Lyndon Johnson signed several important pieces of civil rights legislation into law. Voting rights and housing rights were the focus of the bill. But banks and real estate agents were quick to find loopholes in the bill to keep blacks out of white neighborhoods. White resistance in the South was still fierce. Mobs continued to firebomb, beat, and kill black people. As each brick fell in the wall of discrimination, blood was spilled by white mobs refusing to change.

McLean County Unit #5
Carlock IMC - 105

The Riots

In Northern cities black anger over white police brutality was building to a point of violence. In 1964, riots erupted in Harlem. It was the first of many "long, hot summers" that were to bathe America's cities in blood and fire. In 1965 riots erupted in the Watts neighborhood of Los Angeles. The death toll was 35, with 833 injured and over 3,600 arrested. Fire damage and property losses reached over 200 million dollars.

Major riots began in Chicago and Cleveland in 1966, Newark and Detroit in 1967, and in Chicago, Baltimore, Kansas City, Washington, D.C., and Cleveland in 1968. During each riot, National Guard troops patrolled the streets in full battle gear. Buildings were burned, stores were looted, and snipers shot at police and firemen. Hundreds of innocent people were wounded or killed as tempers flared out of control in the American night.

The Black Muslims

The Black Muslims, or Nation of Islam, started in the black, working-class section of Detroit, Michigan, in the 1930's.

In the late 1950's, Black Muslims set up temples, or mosques, in cities across the country. In a few years, the Muslims developed farming operations in several states. Soon other Muslim business enterprises such as bakeries, clothing stores, and small factories, opened up in black neighborhoods of large cities. The largest black newspaper in the country was run by the Muslims. They also had schools, fleets of airplanes and trucks, office buildings, banks, print shops, and apartment buildings.

Black Power!

By the mid-1960's, many young, black people felt that stronger measures needed to be taken in the struggle for equality. The anger and hopelessness of ghetto life spawned a new political movement. In 1966, the Black Panther Party was formed in California by Huey Newton and Bobby Seale.

One of the main Black Panther programs was feeding breakfasts to schoolchildren. During the breakfasts, the Panthers would tell the children to be proud of themselves and their heritage. The Panthers told the children that "Black is beautiful." At the height of their popularity, the Black Panthers had 1,500 members across the country.

CHAPTER 9
FREEDOM'S LEADERS

Malcolm X — 1925-1965
Civil Rights Activist

Malcolm X was born Malcolm Little in Omaha, Nebraska. He was the seventh of eleven children. Malcolm's father, Reverend Earl Little, was a Baptist minister who was a strong believer in Marcus Garvey's black independence movement. Reverend Little's ideas of black pride upset the local Ku Klux Klan, and his family was driven out of town. The Littles moved to Lansing, Michigan.

Civil rights activist, Malcolm X.

When Malcolm was four years old, a racist group in Lansing burned his house to the ground. Reverend Little rebuilt the home. When Malcolm was six, his father was murdered by thugs. The murder went unpunished by the local police.

After his father's death, Malcolm's life changed for the worse. He quit school in eighth grade and ran away to Boston, Massachusetts, and then to Harlem. Soon he became involved in a life of crime. At age twenty-one, he was sent to prison for six years.

While in prison, Malcolm became interested in the Black Muslim movement. He dropped his last name and began to call himself Malcolm X. Malcolm was released from prison in 1952. For the next twelve years, he taught the Muslim message and organized Muslim churches. Many people were attracted to Malcolm's message and he soon developed a large following.

The success of Malcolm X caused jealousy and resentment within the Black Muslim movement. In December 1963, Malcolm X was kicked out of the Muslim church by its leader, Elijah Muhammad. Malcolm started his own group called the Organization of Afro-American Unity (OAAU).

On February 15, 1965, Malcolm X's house was firebombed. On February 21, he was shot to death at a rally in New York City. Three Black Muslims were convicted of murdering Malcolm X. Thousands of black people mourned the death of Malcolm X. To blacks all over the world, Malcolm was the leader in the revolution against racism and prejudice.

Martin Luther King, Jr. — 1929-1968
Civil Rights Activist

Martin Luther King, Jr., is without a doubt the most famous and respected civil rights leader in America. His intelligence and speaking skills turned a local racial dispute into a worldwide call for black equality and freedom. Martin Luther King's message of peace and equality changed the face of a nation where discrimination and racism were a fact of life for over 300 years.

Martin Luther King, Jr., was born on Janaury 15, 1929. His father was a minister at the Ebenezer Baptist Church in Atlanta, Georgia. His mother was a schoolteacher. King grew up in a middle-class family where both his parents were well-respected professionals.

King gained worldwide fame as the leader of the civil rights movement. In 1958, he wrote his first book *Stride Toward Freedom.*

In the early sixties, King gave support to the youth groups who organized sit-ins and freedom rides. In 1963, he was arrested in Birmingham, Alabama, for demanding an end to the Jim Crow laws.

When King was arrested in Birmingham, he was placed in solitary confinement while white ministers in the area spoke out against the protests. Disappointment in the white ministers caused King to write *The Letter From Birmingham City Jail.*

Dr. Martin Luther King, Jr., in deep thought at a 1967 press conference where he announced he would not be a candidate for the presidential elections.

King told the white ministers of the hatred, the disrespect, the poverty, and the effect that racism has on children. King ended his letter by asking for a peaceful end to segregation. Soon, King was released from jail and the charges against him were dropped.

Martin Luther King Jr., went on to organize the March on Washington and push for the Civil Rights Act in Congress. In 1964, he organized the Mississippi Summer Project to end discrimination in Mississippi. Two thousand students (most of them white) gathered in Mississippi to end racism.

On November 10, 1964, King was given the Nobel Peace Prize. In 1965, King organized religious leaders from all faiths to march in Selma, Alabama, where police had been brutally beating demonstrators. The violence in Selma caused President Lyndon Johnson to gain passage of the Voting Rights Act of 1965. Blacks could no longer be denied the right to vote by prejudiced Southern politicians.

King moved into a run-down apartment on Chicago's south side, to call attention to the housing needs of blacks. He called a rent strike to force slum landlords to fix up apartments.

In 1968, King went to Memphis, Tennessee, to help sanitation workers gain equal rights and better pay. On April 4, King walked out on the balcony of his hotel and was shot to death by James Earl Ray. When news of his death flashed across television screens, riots began in the black neighborhoods of most major American cities.

The death of Dr. King is mourned by many to this day. Without him, no one can say if the civil rights movement would have been as successful as it was. In life as well as in death, Martin Luther King, Jr., set an example for all people who want equality, peace, and justice.

A FINAL WORD

There are thousands of heroes in the black struggle for equal rights. Most of us will never know the stories of their suffering and success. Anyone interested in further reading should visit his or her public library where there are hundreds of books about black history. As many famous black people have said, "Education is the key to freedom and equality."

INDEX